STECK-VAUGHN

Comprehension Skills

SEQUENCE

LEVEL
E

Linda Ward Beech
Tara McCarthy
Donna Townsend

STECK-VAUGHN
C O M P A N Y
A Subsidiary of National Education Corporation

Executive Editor:	Diane Sharpe
Project Editor:	Melinda Veatch
Design Coordinator:	Sharon Golden
Project Design:	Howard Adkins Communications
Cover Illustration:	Rhonda Childress
Photographs:	©Charles Cyr

ISBN 0-8114-7850-5

6 7 8 9 0 VP 02 01 00 99 98

Sequence is about time. It means the order in which things happen. In this book you will practice finding the sequence.

A basketball game follows a sequence. It has a beginning, a middle, and an end. Other games follow a sequence also. What do you think happened before the event shown in this picture? What will happen next? What happens at the beginning of your favorite game? What happens last?

What Is Sequence?

Sequence means time order, or 1-2-3 order. If several things happen in a story, they happen in a sequence. One event happens first, and it is followed by another event.

How to Read for Sequence

You can find the sequence of events in a story by looking for time words, such as *first*, *next*, and *last*. Here is a list of time words:

later	during	days of the week
today	while	months of the year

Try It!

This paragraph tells a story. Try to follow the sequence. Circle all the time words.

◆

George Washington Carver

George Washington Carver was a famous American scientist. He was born in Missouri. Later he went to school in Iowa. Then he became a teacher at the Tuskegee Institute in Alabama. While he was teaching, he also did experiments with crops. He found hundreds of uses for peanuts, sweet potatoes, and soybeans. When he died in 1943, he was known all over the world for his discoveries. Ten years later, the home where he was born became a national monument.

Try putting the events in the paragraph in the order that they happened. What happened first? Write the number **1** on the line by that sentence. Then write the number **2** by the sentence that tells what happened next. Write the number **3** by the sentence that tells what happened last.

◆ Carver made many discoveries. _____

◆ Carver's home became a national monument. _____

◆ Carver became a teacher at the Tuskegee Institute. _____

Practice with Sequence

Here are some practice sequence questions. The first two are already answered. You can do the third one on your own.

_____*C*_____ **1.** When did Carver do experiments with crops?

      A. before he was in Missouri
      B. after he became famous
      C. while he was teaching

The question has the words "experiments with crops." Find those words in the story about Carver. You will find them in the sentence, "While he was teaching, he also did experiments with crops." Find the time word in that sentence. The word is *while*. The words "while he was teaching" are the same as answer **C**, so **C** is correct.

_____*B*_____ **2.** Where did Carver go just before he went to Alabama?

      A. Missouri
      B. Iowa
      C. Tuskegee

Look at the question carefully. Notice the time word *before*. But notice also that the word *just* is there. So the question is asking where Carver went *just before* he went to Alabama. In the story you will find these sentences: "He was born in Missouri. Later he went to school in Iowa. Then he became a teacher at the Tuskegee Institute in Alabama." So answer **B** is correct. Answer **A** tells where he was born, but not where he was *just before* he went to Alabama. Answer **C** is not correct because it is the name of the place where he went in Alabama.

_____ **3.** When did Carver's home become a national monument?

      A. when he lived in Alabama
      B. after he died
      C. while he was teaching

To check your answers, turn to page 62.

Using What You Know

Here are some time words and some examples that show how to use them. Read the examples. Then fill in the blanks to show a sequence of events in your life.

First

First mix the flour and water together.

Getting some ideas about what to write is the first thing an author does.

♦ The first movie I remember seeing was_____

_____

Then

Then in 1519 Cortez left Spain and sailed to Mexico.

The star grows to a giant size, and then it explodes.

♦ Tonight I'll have dinner and then_____

_____

After

After you come to the top of the hill, turn left and go two blocks.

The heaviest rain started after midnight.

♦ Right after I wake up tomorrow, I will _____

_____

Final

The final stop on the Chisholm Trail was Abilene, Kansas.

Finally General Custer's army lost the battle at the Little Bighorn.

♦ The final thing I'll do this weekend is _____

_____

How to Use This Book

In this book you will read 25 stories. Read each story, and then answer the five questions about it.

When you finish reading and answering the questions, check your answers by looking at pages 59 through 62. Fold the answer page to the unit you are checking. Write the number of correct answers in the score box at the top of the page. After you finish all the stories, work through "Think and Apply" on pages 56 through 58.

Hints for Better Reading

◆ Look for time words while you are reading the stories. Remember that sometimes there may not be a time word. Then you must pay attention to the order in which the events in the story are told.

◆ When you finish a story, read each question carefully. Think about the sequence of the events in the story you have just read. Try to find a sentence in the story that tells about the event mentioned in the question. Then look for a time word in that sentence or in a nearby sentence.

◆ As you read the stories, try to imagine the events as if they were part of a movie. Imagine the scenery changing and people talking to each other. Imagine the beginning, the middle, and the end as if they were happening in front of you at a theater.

Challenge Yourself

Try this special challenge. Read each story. Cover the story with a sheet of paper, and try to remember the sequence. Answer the questions without looking back at the story.

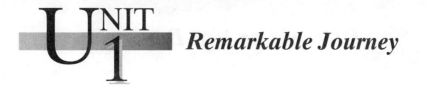

UNIT 1

Remarkable Journey

How does a young dog or cat get to know a new home? The animal uses its nose. Right away it sniffs its new surroundings. Then it makes wider and wider circles, sniffing all the time. Before long it can find its way home very well, even in the dark. It simply follows familiar scents.

But stories exist of animals who found their way across land they had never "sniffed" before. Take the case of Smoky, the Persian cat. Smoky had a funny tuft of red fur under his chin. One day Smoky and his owner began a long journey. They were moving from Oklahoma to Tennessee. When they were just 18 miles from their Oklahoma home, Smoky jumped out of the car. Somehow he found his way back to the old house. There he wandered around outside for many days. Finally he disappeared.

A year later Smoky meowed at the door of a house in Tennessee. A man opened the door. "Is that you, Smoky?" he whispered. At first he couldn't believe it. Then he recognized the tuft of red fur. It was Smoky!

A dog named Bobby also made a remarkable journey. Bobby lived at a farmhouse in a small town in France. One day Bobby's master decided to take him to Paris, 35 miles away. For hours the two wandered through the crowded, noisy city. At the end of the day, when it was time to go home, Bobby's master looked down. The dog had disappeared! The man searched everywhere, but he finally decided that his dog was gone forever, and he sadly went home. Five days later Bobby was barking at the farmhouse door!

Perhaps the most amazing journey of all was made by Prince, a dog who belonged to a British soldier. During World War I, Prince's master was sent to France to fight. After his master left, Prince somehow crossed a wide body of water called the English Channel. Remarkably the dog managed to find his master in the trench where he was fighting.

1. Put these events in the order that they happened. What happened first? Write the number **1** on the line by that sentence. Then write the number **2** by the sentence that tells what happened next. Write the number **3** by the sentence that tells what happened last.

_____ Smoky traveled to Tennessee.

_____ Smoky jumped out of the car.

_____ Smoky went to his old home.

_____ 2. What is the first thing a pet does in a new place?
   A. travels long distances
   B. explores its surroundings
   C. finds its way in the dark

_____ 3. When was the man sure the cat was Smoky?
   A. when he saw the tuft of fur
   B. as soon as he opened the door
   C. before he opened the door

_____ 4. When did the man discover that Bobby was gone?
   A. after 35 miles
   B. five days later
   C. at the end of the day

_____ 5. What did Prince do just before he found his master?
   A. found the British Army
   B. crossed the English Channel
   C. located a trench

UNIT 2

The Thoughtful Gifts

A long time ago in China, two young girls married two brothers. They all lived with the brothers' mother. Although the girls were happy, they greatly missed their own village. They asked many times for permission to return for a visit.

After many years their mother-in-law gave in. However, she told the girls that they must bring her two gifts on their return. Lotus Blossom must bring back fire in a paper package. Moon Flower must bring wind in paper. Without these gifts the girls could not come back to their husbands.

The girls went back to visit their village. But when it was time to return, they began to cry. How could they find the gifts that their mother-in-law demanded? Their younger sister thought about her sisters' problem. At last she had the answer. She gave Lotus Blossom a paper lantern with a candle in it. To Moon Flower she gave a fan. Now the girls could return to their husbands. From then on Lotus Blossom and Moon Flower used thoughts, not tears, to solve their problems.

1. Put these events in the order that they happened. What happened first? Write the number **1** on the line by that sentence. Then write the number **2** by the sentence that tells what happened next. Write the number **3** by the sentence that tells what happened last.

_____ The mother-in-law asked for two gifts.

_____ The girls missed their own village.

_____ The girls married two brothers.

_____ 2. When did the girls ask to visit their village?

    A. before they were married

    B. before they were given permission

    c. when they brought back the presents

_____ 3. When could the girls come back to their husbands?

    A. when they had the gifts

    B. after they asked permission

    c. before they saw their mother

_____ 4. When did the girls cry?

    A. after their sister helped them

    B. while their sister helped them

    c. before their sister helped them

_____ 5. When did the girls live in their own village?

    A. before they married

    B. after they found the gifts

    c. during their marriage

UNIT 3

Pioneer Pilot

In 1926 the aviation industry was just getting started. Only six thousand Americans flew as passengers in planes that year. Most people still thought that flying was just a fast and dangerous sport.

But not everyone thought flying was for the birds. A young woman named Edna Gardner Whyte thought it was important. She thought people would travel by plane in the future. In 1926 Whyte was learning to be a pilot. Most of her teachers told her to quit. They said flying a plane was no job for a woman. But Edna Whyte didn't listen. She went on and got her pilot's license. In fact she got the best score on the test.

This didn't solve all of Edna's problems, though. Most of the airlines did not want a woman for a pilot. Even though she was a good pilot, she couldn't get a job flying planes. She had to keep proving herself again and again. In 1934 she entered a flying race in Maryland. The other pilots laughed at her. They were all men. They didn't laugh when Edna won the race, though. The next year the same race took place. This time a sign said *Men Only*.

Edna went right on flying and winning. In 1937 she won another race. Amelia Earhart handed her the prize. Earhart was also a great pilot. She was the first woman to fly alone across the Atlantic Ocean. Amelia was famous. But Edna Whyte had flown many more hours than Earhart.

Sadly, Earhart disappeared on a flight in 1937. No one ever found her or her plane. But Whyte went on flying until she was in her eighties. She put in more than thirty thousand hours in the air. When she quit racing, she became a teacher. She taught many other people to fly. Her favorite students were young women.

1. Put these events in the order that they happened. What happened first? Write the number **1** on the line by that sentence. Then write the number **2** by the sentence that tells what happened next. Write the number **3** by the sentence that tells what happened last.

_____ Edna Gardner Whyte won a race.

_____ Edna Gardner Whyte learned to fly.

_____ Edna Gardner Whyte got her pilot's license.

_____ **2.** When did teachers tell Edna to quit?
  A. before she took flying lessons
  B. after she taught others
  C. while she was learning to fly

_____ **3.** When did the *Men Only* sign go up in Maryland?
  A. in 1934
  B. in 1935
  C. in 1926

_____ **4.** When did Amelia Earhart disappear?
  A. after she gave Edna Whyte a trophy
  B. at the time she gave Edna Whyte a trophy
  C. before she gave Edna Whyte a trophy

_____ **5.** When did Whyte become a flying teacher?
  A. at the end of her career
  B. at the beginning of her career
  C. before she got her pilot's license

Walt Disney had a problem. He had to make more money. He had made some money in the last two years with his cartoon movie called *Alice in Cartoonland.* But people were getting tired of Alice. He needed an idea for a new character.

Walt sat at his desk drawing circles. A form took shape, and Walt began to get excited. A mouse with big ears and a fat grin appeared. As Walt drew he remembered a mouse named Mortimer that he'd kept as a pet five years earlier. Walt was able to teach Mortimer to do tricks. Mortimer learned to stay inside a circle drawn on a piece of paper. When Mortimer tried to go outside the circle, Walt gently tapped the mouse's nose with a pencil.

Walt finished his picture of a mouse. He put pants, shoes, and gloves on the little guy and showed him to his wife Lillian. She laughed to see a mouse with clothes on. "What are you going to call him?" she wanted to know. "Mortimer," answered Walt. "That's an awful name! You have to think of a better one!" Lillian told him. For days they argued about it. Finally they agreed to call the mouse *Mickey.*

In 1928 Mickey Mouse starred in his own movie. It was called *Steamboat Willie.* People loved the mischievous mouse with three fingers and a wide grin. He was funny, he was cheerful, and he got into innocent trouble.

Since then Mickey Mouse has become one of the most beloved figures in history. He has had his own TV show, fan club, and hat. Leaders of other nations have called Mickey a "symbol of international goodwill." Walt made a lot of money from his idea. He also won an Oscar award for creating Mickey. Now Mickey is over seventy years old. But he still means fun, cheer, and innocence to people around the world.

1. Put these events in the order that they happened. What happened first? Write the number **1** on the line by that sentence. Then write the number **2** by the sentence that tells what happened next. Write the number **3** by the sentence that tells what happened last.

_____ Walt Disney had a problem.

_____ Walt made money from a movie about Alice.

_____ People grew tired of Alice.

_____ 2. When did Walt own a pet mouse named Mortimer?
   A. in 1928
   B. five years before he drew Mickey
   C. when he finished a drawing

_____ 3. When did Walt tap Mortimer's nose?
   A. when a fat grin appeared
   B. when Walt remembered his pet
   C. when Mortimer went outside the circle

_____ 4. How long did Walt and Lillian discuss Mickey's name?
   A. for five years
   B. for days
   C. for two years

_____ 5. When did Walt win an Oscar award?
   A. in 1928
   B. after he created Mickey
   C. when he remembered Mortimer

UNIT 5

Healing Broken Hearts

Many people today have heart trouble. Just fifty years ago people with heart trouble could not get well. Doctors did not know how to help them. Today doctors can help many people with heart trouble. Let's follow Lisa. Lisa has heart trouble.

Lisa went to the hospital Monday morning for tests. Doctors checked her over. They wanted to make sure the rest of her body was well.

Lisa went to a very clean room on Tuesday. She laid down on a table. Then a doctor came in. He gave Lisa medicine so she would not feel anything. Next more doctors came in. They had a long, thin tube with a tiny balloon on one end. They put the tube in Lisa's arm and pushed. They pushed until the end of the tube was in Lisa's heart. After that the doctors used a machine to take a picture of the heart. It showed the trouble. Lisa's heart was stopped up.

Next the doctors blew up the balloon. A doctor slowly moved the tube with the balloon. Pop! The heart was unstopped.

Last the doctors took out the tube. They kept Lisa in the hospital until Saturday. They wanted to make sure she was well. Sunday Lisa started her new, healthy life.

1. Put these things in the order that they happened. What happened first? Write the number **1** on the line by that sentence. Then write the number **2** by the sentence that tells what happened next. Write the number **3** by the sentence that tells what happened last.

_____ Lisa went to a very clean room.

_____ Lisa went to the hospital for tests.

_____ A tube was put in Lisa's heart.

_____ **2.** When did Lisa go to the hospital?
  A. Tuesday morning
  B. Monday
  C. every night

_____ **3.** When did doctors take a picture of Lisa's heart?
  A. Monday morning
  B. after they put the tube in her arm
  C. after they blew up the balloon

_____ **4.** How long did Lisa stay in the hospital?
  A. until Saturday
  B. until Monday
  C. until Sunday

_____ **5.** When did the doctors give Lisa medicine?
  A. before they checked her over
  B. after they unstopped her heart
  C. before they blew up the balloon

The Great Wall of China is amazing. It is the longest wall ever built. It's the one thing made by people that can be seen from the moon. It was built entirely by hand, and it took 1,700 years to complete.

The first ruler of China started building the wall around three thousand years ago. It was slow, hard work, and many workers died. But the workers knew that the wall might protect them someday, so they kept on working.

When the wall was finished, the Chinese people used it for protection. A guard standing on the wall could see enemies coming. The guard then built a fire. Other people could see the smoke during the day and the flames at night. These people built fires, too. Soon the army saw the message of fire and went to fight the enemies. The wall kept out some enemies, but not all of them. The Mongol people, led by Genghis Khan, swept over the wall and into China in the 1200s.

Building the wall took many years. It follows a winding course over hills and mountains and along desert borders. The eastern part of the wall is made of stone blocks and bricks. The inside is filled with earth. The top is wide enough for six horses side by side. Farther west, near the desert, there is not much stone. There the Great Wall is made of packed earth.

Over the years parts of the wall crumbled. Between 1368 and 1644, much of the wall was built again. Most of the wall still standing today comes from this period.

Additional repairs to the wall have been done in this century. Since 1949 three sections have been built again. The Great Wall is an important stop for visitors to China today. It is indeed a most amazing sight.

1. Put these events in the order that they happened. What happened first? Write the number **1** on the line by that sentence. Then write the number **2** by the sentence that tells what happened next. Write the number **3** by the sentence that tells what happened last.

_____ The Great Wall was started.

_____ Much of the wall was rebuilt.

_____ The Mongols swept into China.

_____ 2. When did the first emperor of China live?

    A. in the 1700s

    B. in the 1200s

    C. about three thousand years ago

_____ 3. When did the guard build a fire?

    A. when enemies were coming

    B. after the army came

    C. before the wall was finished

_____ 4. When was the Great Wall recently repaired?

    A. before 1949

    B. during 1949

    C. since 1949

_____ 5. When was part of the Great Wall built again?

    A. before the Mongols came

    B. three thousand years ago

    C. after 1368

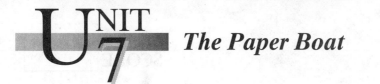
Thor Heyerdahl stared at the old pottery from South America. A slender boat was painted in bright colors on the ancient pot. The boat was made of water plants called reeds. The scientist could not believe what he saw on the pot. The boat painted there was exactly like a boat painted on the pyramids in Egypt. But Egypt was across the Atlantic Ocean. How could people in Egypt and South America have the same boats? Nobody living long ago could cross the ocean in such a small reed boat—or could they?

Thor decided to find the answer to his question. In January he asked people all over Africa and South America how to build reed boats. He found tiny villages where people still built these boats in the ancient way. He hired some boat builders. The people could not read but they built beautiful boats.

It was April and the boat was almost finished. People were laughing at Thor and his reed boat. They called it a paper boat since long ago, people used reeds to make paper. How could a boat built of reeds sail on the ocean?

In May Thor and seven other sailors launched the tiny craft from Egypt. Everyone waited anxiously. It floated. The reeds were yellow and curved up in the front and back. The boat looked like a quarter moon floating on the sea.

The sailors braved the salty ocean. One wave after another rushed towards the little boat. But even when the waves were as tall as five men, the boat glided over the water.

It was July and the boat was approaching South America. Thor was afraid. July was the time for hurricanes, and he hoped they would make it. Suddenly he saw a bird. He knew that birds only flew close to land. Then he saw a ship with happy people on board. They were welcoming the "paper boat" to South America. Thor and his crew had made it. Maybe ancient people really had crossed this great distance in reed boats.

1. Put these events in the order that they happened. What happened first? Write the number **1** on the line by that sentence. Then write the number **2** by the sentence that tells what happened next. Write the number **3** by the sentence that tells what happened last.

_____ Thor hired boat builders.

_____ Thor searched Africa and South America.

_____ Thor found people building boats in the old way.

_____ **2.** When did people laugh at Thor?
- **A.** when the boat was almost finished
- **B.** in May
- **C.** before April

_____ **3.** When was it time for hurricanes?
- **A.** in May
- **B.** when the boat got close to South America
- **C.** when the waves were as tall as five men

_____ **4.** When did Thor see a ship?
- **A.** after the hurricane
- **B.** after he saw the bird
- **C.** in August

_____ **5.** When did Thor realize that reed boats could have crossed the ocean?
- **A.** when he reached South America
- **B.** when he went to Egypt
- **C.** when he built the boat

UNIT 8 — *Meat-Eating Plants*

Sundews are beautiful little plants. They seem so small and harmless. All around the edges of their leaves are tiny hairs that glisten with a shiny liquid. To an insect this liquid looks like food. The insect lands on the leaf. The liquid is sticky and the insect cannot get loose. The sundew wraps itself around the insect and eats it.

Many years ago a scientist named Charles Darwin became fascinated with sundews. Would they eat only insects? Darwin put small bits of roast lamb on the sticky leaves. The plant gobbled them up. Darwin next tried drops of milk, bits of egg, and other foods. The sundew loved them all.

Sundews are just one kind of *meat-eating* plant. These plants trap insects in different ways. Some, like the sundew, use their tiny hairs. Others, like the pitcher plant, have bright colors that attract insects. When an insect lands on the colorful petals, the bug starts falling. The insect slides down into the slippery insides of the plant. At the bottom is a pool of liquid. Special chemicals in this liquid turn the insect into food for the flower.

Bladderworts are meat-eating plants that live mostly in water. Bladderworts have trap doors in their sides. When an insect comes near the tiny hairs on a bladderwort leaf, the trap door opens. The insect is pulled inside.

Some plants collect rain water at their base. When insects go inside to get the water, they cannot escape. The plants are lined with a powder that makes it impossible for the insects to climb back out. Recently a scientist named Durland Fish put four of the plants on a fence around a garden. Within eight days these four plants trapped 136 insects.

1. Put these events in the order that they happened. What happened first? Write the number **1** on the line by that sentence. Then write the number **2** by the sentence that tells what happened next. Write the number **3** by the sentence that tells what happened last.

_____ An insect lands on a sundew leaf.

_____ The sundew wraps itself around the bug.

_____ The sundew's hairs glisten.

_____ 2. When did Darwin become fascinated with sundews?

    A. recently

    B. years ago

    C. within eight days

_____ 3. What did Darwin feed the plant before he fed it milk?

    A. roast lamb

    B. bits of egg

    C. a drinking straw

_____ 4. What happens after the insect slides down into the pitcher plant?

    A. the plant uses its hairs

    B. the insect lands on the petals

    C. the insect becomes food

_____ 5. What happens after an insect lands near a bladderwort's hairs?

    A. the insect slides down

    B. the insect falls into a pool of liquid

    C. the insect is pulled inside

UNIT 9

The Sword and the King

It was time for the yearly tournaments. Young men gathered from all over the country to wrestle and demonstrate their skill with weapons. All the young men would attempt to pull the sword from the stone. The sword had been there for centuries. Its name was Excalibur. The legend was that anyone who could free Excalibur from the stone would be the proper ruler of England. Over the years many had tried. All had failed.

Sir Kay attended this year's tournament with his young cousin Arthur. Arthur's job was to assist Sir Kay with his horse and weapons. When it was time for the sword contests, Sir Kay discovered that his sword was still at home. He was furious.

Arthur remembered the mysterious sword in the stone. "I'll get it for Sir Kay," the youngster thought to himself. While the knights watched in amazement, Arthur easily pulled Excalibur from the stone. All around, people bowed to the boy. Magically, Arthur was now the king of England!

1. Put these events in the order that they happened. What happened first? Write the number **1** on the line by that sentence. Then write the number **2** by the sentence that tells what happened next. Write the number **3** by the sentence that tells what happened last.

_____ Arthur became king.

_____ Arthur had an idea.

_____ Sir Kay left his sword at home.

_____ 2. When were the tournaments held?
- **A.** once a year
- **B.** every other year
- **C.** every century

_____ 3. When was the sword put in the stone?
- **A.** when contests were held
- **B.** yearly
- **C.** many years ago

_____ 4. What happened when Sir Kay left home?
- **A.** he demonstrated his skill
- **B.** he became angry
- **C.** he left his sword

_____ 5. When did people bow?
- **A.** when Sir Kay arrived at the tournament
- **B.** when Arthur had an idea
- **C.** when Arthur pulled the sword from the stone

The Nez Percé are a tribe of Native Americans. They once lived in Oregon, Washington, and Idaho. They lived near the rivers and fished for salmon. In 1840 a young man named Joseph was born. When he grew up, he became Chief Joseph. During this time more and more white settlers moved to his land.

The Nez Percé wanted to live in peace with the settlers. In 1855 they signed a treaty with the United States government. The tribe agreed to give up part of their land and live on a reservation in Oregon.

But in 1860 gold was discovered on the reservation. Gold miners and settlers moved onto the land. In May of 1877, the government ordered all the Nez Percé to move to another reservation, far away in Idaho. The tribe was angry. They didn't want to leave the land of their ancestors.

Some of the chiefs wanted to go to war. But Chief Joseph knew they could not win. He convinced the tribe to travel east. By June 13 they were near the new reservation. Several angry warriors left camp and killed 18 settlers. This act started a war.

For four months the Nez Percé fought and hid in mountains and canyons. They decided to go to Canada, for there the army could not follow them. The tribe stopped to rest near the Bear Paw Mountains in Montana. They were only thirty miles from Canada.

But there the army surrounded the Nez Percé. The tribe fought bravely for five days. But it was winter, and they had no blankets or food. The children were freezing to death. On October 5, 1877, Chief Joseph surrendered.

1. Put these events in the order that they happened. What happened first? Write the number **1** on the line by that sentence. Then write the number **2** by the sentence that tells what happened next. Write the number **3** by the sentence that tells what happened last.

_____ The Nez Percé traveled toward Canada.

_____ Several angry warriors killed 18 settlers.

_____ The government ordered the Nez Percé to move.

_____ **2.** When did the Nez Percé agree to live on a reservation in Oregon?

    A. after Chief Joseph surrendered
    B. when a treaty was signed
    C. after the Nez Percé fought the army

_____ **3.** When was gold discovered on the reservation?

    A. in 1860
    B. when a Nez Percé boy was fishing for salmon
    C. during the summer of 1877

_____ **4.** When were the Nez Percé ordered to move to Idaho?

    A. before the treaty of 1855 was signed
    B. after the 18 settlers were killed
    C. after gold was discovered

_____ **5.** When did Chief Joseph surrender?

    A. after fighting for five days in Montana
    B. while they were in Oregon
    C. on June 13, 1877

UNIT 11

Benjamin Banneker

Benjamin Banneker was born in 1731 near Baltimore. He became the best-known African American of his time. When Benjamin started school he loved it, especially math and science. But his father needed more help around the farm. One day he told Benjamin that he would have to quit school.

Benjamin wanted to continue learning. He decided that he would study on his own. He borrowed books and stayed up late every night reading and doing math problems.

When Benjamin was 22, a merchant loaned him a pocket watch. Benjamin was fascinated! He had heard of clocks but had never seen one. He took the back off and made sketches of the gears. Benjamin decided that he would make his own clock. Carefully he carved the gears out of wood. He studied his sketches and made each part exactly right. The clock kept perfect time for 45 years!

Next Benjamin became interested in the night sky. He noticed that the stars moved. Was there a pattern to this movement? He decided to find out. Each night he sat outside and observed the sky. He made sketches and charts and taught himself astronomy.

The more Benjamin learned, the more he wanted to learn. In 1783, when he was 52, he sold the family farm. Now at last he was able to devote all his time to learning. He taught himself the skill of surveying. In 1791 he helped survey the nation's new capital city, Washington, D. C. That same year he began publishing an almanac. This book predicted the weather and told about the tides. Benjamin printed the almanac for ten years. In spite of his difficult circumstances, Benjamin had followed his dreams. His talent and self-discipline had made it possible for him to accomplish his many goals.

1. Put these events in the order that they happened.
   What happened first? Write the number **1** on the
   line by that sentence. Then write the number **2** by
   the sentence that tells what happened next. Write
   the number **3** by the sentence that tells what
   happened last.

_____ Benjamin sold the family farm.

_____ Benjamin went to school.

_____ Benjamin made a clock based on his sketches.

_____ 2. When did Benjamin first see a watch?
   A. after he wrote the almanac
   B. when he was 22
   C. when he first went to school

_____ 3. When did Benjamin teach himself astronomy?
   A. before he made the clock
   B. while he was in school
   C. before he sold the family farm

_____ 4. When did Benjamin sell the family farm?
   A. before he quit school
   B. before he made the watch
   C. before he learned surveying

_____ 5. When did Benjamin first publish his almanac?
   A. before he made the clock
   B. in 1791
   C. when he was 22

Exploring the Grand Canyon

Major John Wesley Powell had fought in the Civil War. He had lost an arm during a battle. When the war ended, he decided to explore the last unknown land in the United States. He would row down the Colorado River. Powell would be the first explorer to boat through the beautiful but dangerous Grand Canyon.

Powell's party started out on May 24, 1869. The nine men had already spent 72 days on the river by the time they reached the Grand Canyon. On August 4 they floated into its first section, Marble Gorge. This stretch was beautiful but difficult. Many times they had to unload their cargo and lower the boats over rapids by rope. Sometimes they had to carry the boats over the rocky river banks. Often the temperature was a miserable 115 degrees. They were running low on food, and their shoes were in tatters. But the hardest part of the trip still lay ahead.

On August 27 they reached the worst rapids they had seen. Two streams that flowed out of canyons opposite each other had dumped huge boulders into the river. There was no way to go around the raging rapids. The party would have to row through them. Many of the crew doubted that it could be done. One man wrote in his diary that it was "the darkest day of the trip."

After dinner three men came to Powell and told him that they were quitting. They wanted to climb out of the canyon. Powell tried to convince them to stay. But the men were determined to leave. The next morning those men watched as their companions ran the fierce rapids. Somehow the boats passed through the maze of boulders. Today these rapids are still called by the name Powell gave them, Separation Rapids.

At noon on August 29, they finally made it out of the canyon. Powell's daring goal had been reached.

1. Put these events in the order that they happened. What happened first? Write the number **1** on the line by that sentence. Then write the number **2** by the sentence that tells what happened next. Write the number **3** by the sentence that tells what happened last.

_____ They entered Marble Gorge.

_____ Powell fought in the Civil War.

_____ Three men left the group.

_____ **2.** When did Powell lose his arm?

    A. on May 24, 1869

    B. during the Civil War

    C. on the trip through the Grand Canyon

_____ **3.** When did they enter the Grand Canyon?

    A. on August 4, 1869

    B. before the Civil War

    C. after spending a week on the river

_____ **4.** When did they reach Separation Rapids?

    A. on August 29

    B. after they passed Marble Gorge

    C. before they ran low on food

_____ **5.** When did Powell leave the canyon?

    A. on the "darkest day of the trip"

    B. before the crew unloaded the cargo

    C. after they passed through Separation Rapids

UNIT 13 *Giraffes*

Giraffes are the tallest living animals. Most adult giraffes are tall enough to look into second-story windows. Their long necks help them get leaves and fruit that no other animal can reach. Let's see how a giraffe's life begins.

A female giraffe, or cow, gives birth to a baby 15 months after mating. The mother searches for a safe place to give birth. Both the baby, or calf, and the mother are in a great deal of danger right after the birth. More than half of all baby giraffes are killed by lions, cheetahs, or hyenas minutes after they are born.

The new baby drops the 5 feet from its mother to the ground with a thud. It weighs about 130 pounds and is 6 feet tall. The baby can run and jump 10 hours after it is born, but it cannot outrun an enemy.

The mother hides the calf in tall grass. Then she goes to search for food. The baby is fairly safe as long as it stays still. The cow returns to nurse the baby. The calf stays hidden for about a month.

After a month the mother and baby join a group of four or five other cows with their calves. The calves stay together while their mothers gather food. Sometimes one mother stays with them. The cows return at night to protect the calves. The calves stay in this group until they are about a year old.

By the time they are a year old, the giraffes are 10 to 12 feet tall. They can outrun all of their enemies except the cheetah. And it rarely attacks an animal larger than itself. Giraffes continue to grow until they are 7 or 8 years old. Adults are between 14 and 18 feet tall.

1. Put these events in the order that they happened. What happened first? Write the number **1** on the line by that sentence. Then write the number **2** by the sentence that tells what happened next. Write the number **3** by the sentence that tells what happened last.

_____ The baby can run and jump.

_____ The baby drops five feet to the ground.

_____ The female giraffe looks for a safe place to give birth.

_____ 2. When does a female giraffe give birth?
   A. after she joins a group of other cows
   B. every year
   C. 15 months after mating

_____ 3. When are the mother and baby in danger?
   A. 10 hours after the baby's birth
   B. right after the baby's birth
   C. 15 months after the baby's birth

_____ 4. When do the cow and calf join a group of other females and babies?
   A. about a month after the baby is born
   B. when the calf is a year old
   C. when the calf is 7 or 8 years old

_____ 5. When do giraffes stop growing?
   A. when they are 10 or 12 years old
   B. when they are 7 or 8 years old
   C. when they join a group of other giraffes

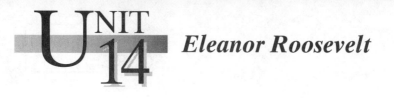

Eleanor Roosevelt was born in 1884. The Roosevelts were one of New York's leading families. They were wealthy and moved among people in high society. But in spite of all this, Eleanor did not have a happy childhood. At the age of eight, both her mother and a brother died of illness. Two years later, her father died in an accident. Eleanor was filled with sadness.

When she was 15, Eleanor went to school near London. For the first time, she came alive. Her sharp mind and curious nature were praised. She was friendly and willing to help others. This made her popular with the other girls. Here she was taught to use her influence to help other people. Eleanor learned this lesson well. For the rest of her life, she tried to serve others.

When Eleanor was 18, she came back to New York. There she started dating her distant cousin, Franklin D. Roosevelt. When she was 21, they were married. For the next ten years, Eleanor devoted herself to her family. In those ten years, she had five children. During this time Franklin became a state senator. Eleanor became interested in politics, too. During World War I, she did volunteer work. She became active in the Democratic party. Eleanor grew very independent.

In 1921 Franklin became ill with polio. He was affected by the disease for the rest of his life. Eleanor helped him continue his career. She made fact-finding trips for him. In 1928 Franklin became governor of New York.

In 1932 Franklin was elected president. Eleanor became one of the most active first ladies ever. She gave lectures and wrote articles. She worked for equal rights for minorities. She became well known for her efforts to help all people.

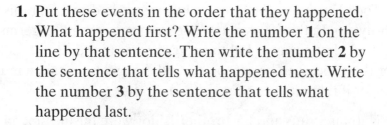
1. Put these events in the order that they happened. What happened first? Write the number **1** on the line by that sentence. Then write the number **2** by the sentence that tells what happened next. Write the number **3** by the sentence that tells what happened last.

_____ Eleanor became active in the Democratic party.

_____ Eleanor had five children.

_____ Eleanor became first lady of the country.

_____ 2. When did Eleanor's mother die?
  A. after Eleanor's father died
  B. before Eleanor went to London
  C. after Eleanor married Franklin

_____ 3. When did Eleanor go to school near London?
  A. after her mother died
  B. before her brother died
  C. when her father died

_____ 4. When did Eleanor get married?
  A. after World War I
  B. after Franklin became ill with polio
  C. after she came back from London

_____ 5. When did her husband become president?
  A. when Eleanor was 21
  B. after he was governor of New York
  C. before he became ill

UNIT 15 *Safe Milk*

Today we know the milk we buy is safe to drink. But this wasn't always so. In the 1800s many diseases were spread by germs in milk. At last a way to kill these germs was found. But it took years for this process to be accepted. And it might have taken much longer if it hadn't been for Nathan Straus.

Nathan Straus and his brother Isidor were businessmen in New York City. They owned Macy's Department Store. Nathan Straus had read about Louis Pasteur. Pasteur had developed a way of heating milk to kill germs that cause disease. His method was called pasteurization. Straus became convinced that all milk should be pasteurized. His fight to convince others took twenty years.

In 1891 the first pasteurizer was put in a milk plant in the United States. But some people fought this idea. Dairy farmers didn't want to buy the machine. Other people didn't think it was necessary. They thought keeping cows clean was enough to make milk safe.

In New York City, one child in ten died before the age of five. Straus was convinced that bad milk was one of the causes. He wanted to help. In 1893 he set up a stand and sold pasteurized milk in a poor neighborhood. He sold the milk for a low price. Many people bought milk there. The young children in the neighborhood became healthier. Few of them died. In the next few years, Straus set up 12 more stands.

In 1907 Straus and others wanted a law passed that would force milk producers to pasteurize milk. But those who sold milk were against the law. It was voted down. Straus kept fighting. He gave speeches, wrote letters, and spoke to the city leaders. Finally pasteurization was accepted. By 1914, 95 percent of New York City's milk supply was pasteurized. The death rate of young children dropped almost at once. In 1923 Straus was given an award for his efforts to help the people of New York City.

1. Put these events in the order that they happened. What happened first? Write the number **1** on the line by that sentence. Then write the number **2** by the sentence that tells what happened next. Write the number **3** by the sentence that tells what happened last.

_____ Straus wanted to stop the sale of unsafe milk.

_____ Louis Pasteur found a way to kill the germs in milk.

_____ Straus was given an award for his public service.

_____ 2. When were many diseases spread by milk?

    A. after Straus received his award
    B. before pasteurization was accepted
    C. in 1914

_____ 3. When was pasteurization developed?

    A. after the child death rate went down
    B. after Straus spoke to the city leaders
    C. before Straus started selling milk

_____ 4. When did Straus set up his first milk stand?

    A. after the first pasteurizer was used in America
    B. before he owned Macy's
    C. after he was given a public-service award

_____ 5. When did the child death rate drop?

    A. before Straus fought for pasteurization
    B. soon after most of the city's milk was pasteurized
    C. in 1891

Would you like to step back in time? If so you might enjoy a trip to Mesa Verde National Park. Mesa Verde is in southwestern Colorado. Spanish explorers gave this region its name. *Mesa verde* means "green plateau." It became a national park in 1906.

Scientists have studied the region and have learned a great deal about the people who lived there. They called them the Anasazi, or "old ones." We know that about 1200 the Anasazi built their homes in the caves of the canyon walls. They used stone blocks to build apartment-like dwellings. When you see them, it is easy to pretend you are one of the people who lived there centuries ago.

Spring was a busy time for the Anasazi. The women cleaned the walls of their homes and painted designs on them. They made new pots and bowls out of clay. The men got ready for spring planting. They performed a ceremony with different colors of corn seed. They prayed for four days, and then they planted their fields. In the summer the men took care of the crops. They weeded and chased away deer, squirrels, and birds. The women made many trips to the springs below to get water. They also gathered wild plants. They used these for medicine and food.

In the fall everyone picked the crops. They carried the corn, squash, and beans to their cliff dwellings. Without this food the Anasazi would have starved during the long winter months. The cold weather and snow made winters hard for the cliff dwellers. They spent much time near a fire in their homes. They also spent time in the kiva, or ceremonial room.

About 1300 the Anasazi left their homes in the canyons. No one knows why they left or where they went. Luckily the cliff dwellings are still here for us to explore. Maybe someday someone will find the answer.

1. Put these events in the order that they happened. What happened first? Write the number **1** on the line by that sentence. Then write the number **2** by the sentence that tells what happened next. Write the number **3** by the sentence that tells what happened last.

_____ The Anasazi moved into the caves in the canyons.

_____ The Anasazi harvested food for the winter.

_____ The Anasazi left their homes in the canyons.

_____ **2.** When did Mesa Verde become a national park?
   A. when the Spanish explorers gave it its name
   B. before the Anasazi painted designs on their walls
   C. after the Anasazi left their homes on the cliffs

_____ **3.** When did the Anasazi move into the caves?
   A. in 1906
   B. about 1200
   C. about 1300

_____ **4.** When did the Anasazi plant their crops?
   A. after having a ceremony with corn seed
   B. before praying for four days
   C. after chasing away deer, squirrels, and birds

_____ **5.** When did the Anasazi pick the crops?
   A. in the spring
   B. before they built their cave homes
   C. before winter

UNIT 17

A Maori Legend

New Zealand is a beautiful country on the other side of the world from the United States. The native people are called the Maori. The Maori tell their children many legends about how things came to be the way they are.

This story is about Maui, an important figure in Maori legends. Maui was half god and half person. He often heard the people in his village complain about how short the days were. They woke up very early to fish and hunt. But no matter how they tried, they couldn't get all their work done before the sun set.

Maui thought about this problem, and at last he came up with an idea. He called the villagers together. "I have a plan," he said. He asked the women to gather flax. "Very good," Maui told them after they had gathered enough flax plants. "Now take these plants and weave a huge net." The people worked for many days, until at last Maui announced that the net was large enough.

Maui and the men from the village took the net and traveled east. They found the cave where the sun was spending the night. The men covered themselves with mud as protection from the sun's heat. Then they stretched the net over the cave's entrance. When they saw the first rays of light the next morning, they grasped the net tightly.

Trapped the sun roared in anger and struggled to get free. The men felt its powerful heat. Maui ran toward the sun and began attacking it with his magic ax. The sun was furious! "What are you trying to do? Kill me?" it asked. "No," answered Maui. "But we want you to move across the sky slower. We can't get all our work done before you set!" When the sun agreed to journey across the sky more slowly, the men released the net and let the sun go. From then on the days were as long as they are now. The people were happy. Now they had enough time to finish all their work.

1. Put these events in the order that they happened. What happened first? Write the number **1** on the line by that sentence. Then write the number **2** by the sentence that tells what happened next. Write the number **3** by the sentence that tells what happened last.

_____ Maui attacked the sun with an ax.

_____ The men stretched a net over the cave's entrance.

_____ Maui asked the women to gather flax.

_____ **2.** When did the villagers weave a net?

    A. after the men went to the cave

    B. after Maui attacked the sun with his ax

    C. after the women gathered the flax

_____ **3.** When did Maui share his plan with the villagers?

    A. after the men wove a net and traveled east

    B. after he heard the villagers complain

    C. at different times each day

_____ **4.** When did the men cover their faces with mud?

    A. before Maui told the people his plan

    B. before they went to the cave

    C. before the net was woven

_____ **5.** When did the men let the sun go?

    A. as soon as it roared

    B. when it agreed to travel more slowly

    C. when Maui told them to

UNIT 18

Changes in Farming

What job would you have had if you had lived in England in 1540? Chances are you would have been a farmer. Most people were. It took many people to raise enough food. Now just two out of one hundred people in England farm. The rest work in towns and cities. This pattern is true in many parts of the world. What allowed so many people to leave the farm?

Several discoveries and inventions caused this change. One of these was rotating, or changing, crops. Farmers had long known that growing the same crop in the same field year after year made the soil poor. So they usually left fields empty part of the time.

In the early 1700s, Charles Townshend found a way to rotate four crops. This way fields could be used all year. For example, four fields would be planted with wheat, clover, barley, and turnips. By rotating the crop grown in each field every year, the soil remained rich. Grasslands that could not be used before could now be farmed. This rotation system allowed farmers to raise much more food, both for themselves and their animals.

Robert Bakewell was an English farmer in the late 1700s. He wanted to raise better farm animals. He produced better horses, cattle, and sheep. He developed a sheep that could be raised for meat as well as wool.

The invention of new farm tools also led to great change. About 1700 the seed drill was invented. Before that time seeds were scattered by hand. The seed drill dug trenches in the dirt and planted the seeds. This tool was the first modern farm machine. Crop rotation, better farm animals, and new farm tools made it possible for fewer people to produce a lot of food. Thousands of families moved from farms to the cities.

1. Put these events in the order that they happened. What happened first? Write the number **1** on the line by that sentence. Then write the number **2** by the sentence that tells what happened next. Write the number **3** by the sentence that tells what happened last.

_____ Townshend developed a system of crop rotation.

_____ The seed drill was invented.

_____ Thousand of families moved to cities.

_____ 2. When were most people farmers?
   A. in the 1980s
   B. after the invention of the seed drill
   C. in 1540

_____ 3. When were seeds scattered by hand?
   A. during the 1900s
   B. before the seed drill was invented
   C. during the winter

_____ 4. When were better farm animals developed?
   A. during the late 1700s
   B. before Townshend lived
   C. after peole moved to the cities

_____ 5. When was the seed drill invented?
   A. in 1540
   B. after crop rotation was developed
   C. before Bakewell produced better animals

UNIT 19

Captain Cook's First Voyage

James Cook became one of the most famous explorers of all time. But when he was chosen to be captain of the *Endeavor,* he was unknown. The *Endeavor* was being sent to Tahiti. Scientists and artists would watch Venus pass between Earth and the sun from a spot in Tahiti. The ship set sail from England on August 25, 1768.

The ship sailed east across the Atlantic, then down the coast of South America. It passed around Cape Horn. Then it sailed through the Pacific. Cook and his crew spent weeks in Tahiti. They enjoyed the lovely island. On June 3, 1769, they watched the passage of Venus. Their instruments carefully recorded the event.

With great excitement Captain Cook read his secret orders for the rest of the trip. He was to search for an unknown continent in the southern hemisphere. If he found it, he was to claim the land for England. The *Endeavor* left Tahiti on July 13, 1769.

Cook sailed until he reached the beautiful land of New Zealand. He sailed around the two islands. He claimed the new land for England. From there he sailed west until he reached Australia. This he also claimed for England. The *Endeavor* sailed north along the coast for two thousand miles. Cook made careful maps of the coastline. The scientists made sketches of the plants and animals. Perhaps the most surprising sight was the kangaroo!

Finally it was time to go back to England. But to do so, the *Endeavor* had to sail through dangerous waters. On June 10, 1770, the ship ran into a rocky reef and was badly damaged. Water flooded the ship. Cook ordered everything heavy to be thrown overboard. This lightened the ship enough so that it could float off the reef. They managed to sail to shore, but it took them six weeks to make the repairs. The ship made the slow trip home. After almost three years of ocean travel, the *Endeavor* arrived in England on July 12, 1771.

1. Put these events in the order that they happened. What happened first? Write the number **1** on the line by that sentence. Then write the number **2** by the sentence that tells what happened next. Write the number **3** by the sentence that tells what happened last.

_____ The *Endeavor* was badly damaged.

_____ Cook mapped the New Zealand coast.

_____ The *Endeavor* was sent to Tahiti.

_____ 2. When did the *Endeavor* leave England?

    A. after they had reached Tahiti

    B. before Cook became famous

    C. after Cook made his maps

_____ 3. When did the crew watch Venus?

    A. before they left England

    B. when they passed Cape Horn

    C. before they sailed to Australia

_____ 4. When did Cook reach Australia?

    A. after he sailed around New Zealand

    B. after the ship was badly damaged

    C. before he went to Tahiti

_____ 5. When did the *Endeavor* return to England?

    A. when Cook was chosen to be the ship's captain

    B. six weeks after they left Tahiti

    C. after the damages to the ship were repaired

1988 is a year that will not be forgotten for a long time at Yellowstone National Park. Fires broke out in June and burned fiercely until September. The flames were not put out completely until November. They covered almost half of the huge park. What caused such huge fires? There are several answers to this question.

Lodgepole pines make up eighty percent of the park's forests. These trees grow quickly. But they only live about two hundred years. Then many of the pines die and are blown down by high winds. The trees lie on the forest floor for many years. In wet forests they would rot and turn back into soil. But it is too dry for this to happen in Yellowstone. In 1988 dead wood covered the forest floor.

Yellowstone usually gets a lot of snow in the winter. When the snow melts, it provides water for the plants. But for six winters in the 1980s, little snow had fallen. Rain also usually falls during the summer months. But 1988 was the driest summer in 116 years.

Several fires started in and near the park in June. Park officials fought the fires caused by human carelessness. But they didn't try to put out the fires started by lightning. They knew that fires help clean out the dead wood. But when little rain fell in June and July, the fires became larger and larger. Over 17,000 acres had burned by July 21. Park officials decided that it was time to fight the roaring fires.

On June 23 strong winds blew the fires into new areas of the park. Firefighters battled the blazes. But they had little success. On August 20 eighty mile-per-hour winds swept through the park. This day became known as Black Saturday. Fires that had almost died out came back to life. No matter how hard the firefighters tried, they couldn't control the flames. But snow and rain began to fall in September. Then the worst of the fires were put out. The remaining fires were put out by heavy snows in November.

1. Put these events in the order that they happened. What happened first? Write the number **1** on the line by that sentence. Then write the number **2** by the sentence that tells what happened next. Write the number **3** by the sentence that tells what happened last.

_____ Yellowstone had the driest summer in 116 years.

_____ The worst of the fires were put out.

_____ Several fires started in the park.

_____ **2.** When did the fires begin in Yellowstone?

    A. when the trees began to die

    B. when the heavy snows fell

    C. before the strong winds blew in

_____ **3.** When did little snow fall in the park?

    A. during the 1980s

    B. in November

    C. 116 years ago

_____ **4.** When did park officials decide to fight the fires?

    A. when lightning struck

    B. after 17,000 acres had burned

    C. on Black Sunday

_____ **5.** When was Black Saturday?

    A. when the trees died

    B. one month before the first fires started

    C. when strong winds hit the park

Have you ever seen a person in a top hat and black suit with a long wire brush? If so you may have seen a chimney sweep. Chimney sweeps have been around for hundreds of years.

The first chimneys were built in the 1100s. At first only rich people could afford them. But by the 1500s, fireplaces were common in English homes. Most houses had one or more chimneys. The chimneys had to be cleaned or the fireplaces would not work properly. Dirty chimneys could cause fires. Many countries passed laws that required chimneys to be cleaned once or twice a year. Chimney sweeping became a regular profession.

Life was hard for chimney sweeps in England in the 1700s. Tall, narrow houses were built in the cities. Chimneys were designed to take up as little space as possible. They were too small for adults to climb into. So many sweeps hired young boys as helpers, or apprentices. These boys were not treated well. They spent long hours climbing into dirty chimneys. Most of the time, they were not given enough food or warm clothing. In 1788 a law was passed that said sweeps could not be younger than eight.

In 1803 an English gentleman became concerned about these boys. He formed a society to try and help them. The society held hearings to find out more about the problem. They decided that children should not have to clean chimneys. They offered a reward to anyone who could invent a chimney-sweeping machine. George Smart invented a machine with a large, round brush. The brush fit on a hollow stick. More sticks could be added to make it longer.

In 1804 the society went to Parliament. They wanted a bill passed that would outlaw the use of children as sweeps. They said the new sweeping brush could be used instead. But Parliament did not pass the law. In 1833 the age of apprentices was raised from 8 to 10. Finally in 1840 a law was passed that allowed only those who were 21 or older to work as chimney sweeps.

1. Put these events in the order that they happened. What happened first? Write the number **1** on the line by that sentence. Then write the number **2** by the sentence that tells what happened next. Write the number **3** by the sentence that tells what happened last.

_____ A sweeping machine was invented.

_____ An English gentleman formed a society to help sweeps.

_____ Sweeps hired young boys as apprentices.

_____ 2. When were the first chimneys built?

    A. after tall, narrow houses became popular
    B. when George Smart was a child
    C. before chimney sweeping became a regular job

_____ 3. When was the sweeping machine invented?

    A. when child chimney sweeps began to be used
    B. after a reward was offered
    C. before fireplaces became common in England

_____ 4. When was life hard for the sweeps?

    A. when chimneys became too small
    B. when only rich people could afford chimneys
    C. when a law was passed requiring clean chimneys

_____ 5. When was a group formed to help the young sweeps?

    A. when a law forbidding child sweeps was passed
    B. when the legal age was raised from eight to ten
    C. when a man became worried about their safety

UNIT 22

The History of Kites

No one knows when the first kite was made. But the first record of a kite was over 2000 years ago in China. General Han Hsin was the leader of a rebel army. He wanted to overthrow a cruel king. But he only had a few men. Hsin decided to dig a tunnel into the king's castle. He flew a kite to determine how long the tunnel should be. The men in the tunnel took the kite string with them. When they reached the end of the string, they knew to dig up. They came up in the castle courtyard and defeated the king.

Kites have been flown in Japan for hundreds of years. In the 1700s kites were flown in the fall to give thanks for a good harvest. Stalks of rice were tied to the kites. Kites were also flown to send good wishes to couples who had had their first son.

Today in Japan kites are often flown as part of a celebration, such as the beginning of a new year. The kites are painted to look like animals, heroes, and gods. Small kites as well as huge ones are made. Kite festivals are held each year in many regions of the country.

Kites have been used for scientific purposes in the western world. Most people have heard of Benjamin Franklin and his kite. Franklin had been studying electricity. He thought that lightning was a form of electricity, but he wasn't sure. In 1752 he tried to find out. He flew a kite in a storm. A key was attached to the kite. When sparks jumped from the key, it proved his idea was correct.

In the 1890s Lawrence Hargrave invented the box kite. He used this kite to test ideas about flight. From 1898 until 1933, the United States Weather Bureau used box kites to gather weather data. The Wright Brothers also experimented with kites. What they learned helped them make the first airplane flight in 1903.

1. Put these events in the order that they happened. What happened first? Write the number **1** on the line by that sentence. Then write the number **2** by the sentence that tells what happened next. Write the number **3** by the sentence that tells what happened last.

_____ Franklin discovered that lightning was electricity.

_____ Han Hsin used a kite to measure distance.

_____ The Wright brothers experimented with kites.

_____ 2. When was the first record of a kite?
   A. one hundred years ago
   B. before Benjamin Franklin was born
   C. before General Han Hsin was born

_____ 3. When were kites often flown in Japan?
   A. before a good harvest
   B. after the birth of a first son
   C. during storms

_____ 4. When did Franklin fly a kite in a storm?
   A. before the cruel king was defeated
   B. before the Wrights experimented with kites
   C. when he studied electricity

_____ 5. When did the Weather Bureau use kites?
   A. after the invention of the box kite
   B. before the Wright brothers made their first plane
   C. before Benjamin Franklin studied electricity

Once a little girl named Mashen'ka went into the forest with her friends. The girls were picking berries and didn't realize how far they had gone. Suddenly a bear grabbed Mashen'ka and carried her away. The other girls ran back to the village and told what had happened. Mashen'ka's parents were heartbroken because they were sure the bear had eaten their only child.

But the bear wasn't hungry; he was lonely. He wanted someone to keep him company. He made Mashen'ka a bed of moss and brought her honey to eat. But Mashen'ka knew her family was worried, so she sat and cried a lot of the time.

"Why are you crying?" the bear asked. "Wouldn't you cry if your parents thought you had been eaten up?" she replied sadly. "Don't worry, I'll go and check on them tonight," the bear said. "Here is some flour to make them some pies." Mashen'ka made the pies and told the bear not to eat any of them. "If you eat any, I will be very angry," she said. Then she hid in the bottom of the basket and put the pies on top of her.

That evening the bear picked up the basket and started towards the village. But it was heavy, and the bear grew tired. He started to sit down and have a snack. But a loud voice said, "Don't you dare take a seat nor a little pie eat!" The bear was surprised. But he continued his journey. At midnight the bear knocked on the door of Mashen'ka's house. But just as her father opened the door, the village dogs chased the bear away. Mashen'ka jumped out of the basket and hugged her parents. They had a joyful reunion!

A week later the bear again knocked on the door. He said, "I have come to say good-bye. I must go away. I forgive you for running away, and I've brought you something to remember me by." Then he gave her a heavy bag full of gold and silver. Mashen'ka and her family were rich for the rest of their lives!

1. Put these events in the order that they happened. What happened first? Write the number **1** on the line by that sentence. Then write the number **2** by the sentence that tells what happened next. Write the number **3** by the sentence that tells what happened last.

_____ The bear gave Mashen'ka gold and silver.

_____ Mashen'ka and her friends were picking berries.

_____ The bear brought Mashen'ka honey to eat.

_____ **2.** When did the bear grab Mashen'ka?

    A. when she was making pies

    B. when she was hugging her parents

    C. when she was picking berries in the woods

_____ **3.** When were Mashen'ka's parents sad?

    A. when her friends told them what had happened

    B. when Mashen'ka jumped out of the basket

    C. when the bear returned

_____ **4.** When did Mashen'ka make the pies?

    A. when she was given honey to eat

    B. before the bear went to visit her parents

    C. after she hid in the basket

_____ **5.** When did Mashen'ka jump out of the basket?

    A. before the bear brought her gold and silver

    B. when the bear started to eat a pie

    C. before dogs chased the bear away

UNIT 24 *Dolphins*

For centuries dolphins have been thought of as special animals. Plutarch, a Greek writer, praised their friendliness two thousand years ago. Scenes of people riding on dolphins have appeared in the art of many countries.

There are more than 38 kinds of dolphins. Most types live in the ocean. They are related to whales. Dolphins are very smart. They can learn, remember, and solve problems. They are born entertainers who love to perform. You can see them do tricks at marine amusement parks.

Dolphins travel in herds. They are social animals who like to play. They often toss seaweed and driftwood up in the air. Dolphins become very unhappy and lonely if they are separated from their companions. Dolphins mate in the spring. A baby is born a year later. The other dolphins surround the mother while she is giving birth. They do this to protect her from danger. Soon after birth the mother pushes the baby to the surface so that it can breathe. The baby nurses, or drinks the mother's milk, for about 18 months. The mother teaches the baby and protects it from harm.

Many tales have been told of dolphins helping people. One famous dolphin was named Pelorus Jack. Jack lived in Cook's Strait between the North Island and South Island of New Zealand. From 1888 until the 1920s, Jack guided ships through Cook's Strait. People came from around the world to see him.

In 1978 a small fishing boat was lost off the coast of South Africa. It was caught in a thick fog and dangerous water. The fishermen told of four dolphins who led their boat to shore. Another newspaper account told of a ship that exploded. A woman was injured and thrown overboard. She said three dolphins swam near her and helped her float. They stayed with her until she could climb on a buoy. There are many other stories of dolphins saving drowning people by pushing them to shallow water.

1. Put these events in the order that they happened. What happened first? Write the number **1** on the line by that sentence. Then write the number **2** by the sentence that tells what happened next. Write the number **3** by the sentence that tells what happened last.

_____ The baby nurses for about 18 months.

_____ The mother pushes the baby to the surface.

_____ The other dolphins surround the mother.

_____ 2. When did Plutarch praise dolphins?
   A. three hundred years ago
   B. in 1888
   C. two thousand years ago

_____ 3. When do other dolphins surround a mother dolphin?
   A. after the mother dolphin gives birth
   B. after the mother nurses her baby
   C. after the mother pushes her baby to the surface

_____ 4. When did Pelorus Jack guide ships through Cook's Strait?
   A. before Plutarch died
   B. before four dolphins helped some lost fishermen
   C. before dolphins were thought of as special animals

_____ 5. When was a small fishing boat lost off the coast of South Africa?
   A. during the time when Pelorus Jack guided ships
   B. when a woman's ship exploded
   C. in 1978

UNIT 25 *Boomerangs*

Boomerangs are one of the world's oldest weapons. They have been around for thousands of years. Scientists say that one boomerang they found was 2,400 years old. Boomerangs were invented before the bow and arrow.

The boomerang is often thought of in connection with Australia. But boomerangs were used in Asia, Europe, and Africa, too. Many people used a curved throwing stick to hunt with. But the native people known as the Australian Aborigines are the only people who made a boomerang that comes back.

The Aborigines had three types of boomerangs. One was used in ceremonies. It was carved with designs and treated with respect. The second kind was a nonreturning boomerang. This type was used for hunting. It could kill a bird or small animal. Thrown just right it could knock out a kangaroo. The best-known kind was the returning boomerang. This was used mainly for games and sports. Sometimes it was used to catch birds. The men would stretch nets in the trees. Then they would throw a boomerang over a flock of ducks or parakeets. The birds would mistake the boomerang for a hawk and fly into the nets.

James Cook was the first explorer to see the Australian boomerang. In 1770 he described the strange flying sticks. The boomerang's name probably came from a word that meant "wind." No one knows how the returning boomerang was invented. But scientists guess that it was developed when hunters accidentally made a curved throwing stick that came back.

Boomerangs are curved like a plane's wing on the top. They are flat on the bottom. This design helps them lift in the wind. The first person to explain why a boomerang returns was T. L. Mitchell. He was a scientist who wrote a paper about it in 1842.

1. Put these events in the order that they happened. What happened first? Write the number **1** on the line by that sentence. Then write the number **2** by the sentence that tells what happened next. Write the number **3** by the sentence that tells what happened last.

_____ Captain Cook saw boomerangs.

_____ The Australian Aborigines used boomerangs.

_____ T. L. Mitchell wrote a paper on boomerangs.

_____ 2. When were boomerangs invented?
   A. before James Cook traveled to Australia
   B. millions of years ago
   C. after the bow and arrow

_____ 3. When did the Aborigines use boomerangs?
   A. after they had stretched nets in the trees
   B. after they played games and sports
   C. after hawks flew by

_____ 4. When did Cook first see boomerangs?
   A. when he went hunting
   B. before Mitchell studied boomerangs
   C. thousands of years ago

_____ 5. When did someone first explain why a boomerang returns?
   A. when the bow and arrow was invented
   B. when Captain Cook traveled to Australia
   C. after the Aborigines used boomerangs for hunting

Think and Apply

Timely Directions

Write silly directions for one of the activities named in the box. Divide your directions into steps. Some activities will take six steps, and some will take fewer. Use your imagination, and remember to give your steps a specific order.

How to kill time	How to waste time
How to juggle time	How to lose time
How to manage time	How to spend time

Example: How to make a timekeeper

1. First get a shoebox with a lid.
2. Then paint the box your favorite color.
3. Next put your watch in the box.
4. Also put your calendar in the box.
5. At midnight put the lid on the box.
6. Finally put the box in a safe place.

Your Directions: _____

1. _____
2. _____
3. _____
4. _____
5. _____
6. _____

Night into Day

Read the paragraph. Decide what Peggy probably did at each time listed. Write your answers on the lines below.

Peggy Johnson is a firefighter. She begins her shift at midnight and works for eight hours at a time. The first thing she does when she arrives at work is sign in. Then she inspects the fire engine, making sure it runs well and has plenty of gas. Then she inspects her hat, coat, and other fire-fighting equipment. In the middle of the shift, Peggy eats dinner. Last Saturday when the bell sounded an hour before her shift was over, Peggy went to fight the fire. The fire lasted three hours. When Peggy returned to the station, she was so exhausted that she fell asleep there. She finally woke up at noon and went home.

Last Saturday's Schedule

Midnight _____

12:05 a.m. _____

12:10 a.m. _____

12:30 a.m. _____

4:00 a.m. _____

7:00 a.m. _____

10:00 a.m. _____

Noon _____

To check your answers, turn to page 62.

Events in a Tiger's Day

Here is a story about a tiger. It is in the wrong order. Write out the story on the lines below. Put the sentences in the right order. When you have finished, check your answer on page 62.

The Tiger

Then the tiger suddenly sprang up and raced to catch its lunch. It was early in the morning when the tiger woke up. As it walked across the grass, the tiger saw a deer. After its meal the big cat laid under the tree and thoroughly cleaned its fur. The big cat began its day by looking for something to eat. The big cat crouched down so that it could look around without being seen. Before eating the deer, the tiger pulled it into the shade of a tree.

_____

_____

_____

_____

_____

_____

_____

_____

_____

_____

_____

_____

To check your answers, turn to page 62.